Acknowledgements

First and foremost, we would like to thank ALL of our students, both past and present, for their help and feedback on the questions that follow. We are very grateful to you all!

Also, we would like to thank our friends and family for all their encouragement, especially Mike Patteson and Emma Jolly, who have been a constant support to us.

Charlie Boad and Kate Bridges, 2009

www.luckygecko.com

© Lucky Gecko 2009

All rights reserved. No part of this publication may be photocopied, reproduced, stored or transmitted in any form or by any means without written permission of the publisher. Any breach of copyright may result in prosecution.

11+ Verbal Reasoning Multiple Choice Practice Questions

Book 1

Charlie Boad and Kate Bridges

© Lucky Gecko 2009

Useful Information for Parents

Verbal Reasoning is used across the country in numerous 11+, Common Entrance and Secondary School Selection tests.

This book provides excellent foundation work for some of the most commonly used question types and is most effective when completed before attempting papers under timed conditions. It is therefore recommended that students work through the questions at their own pace, in order to ensure that they feel confident in their methods before having to worry about speed.

If you would like your child to practice completing questions within a time limit, please see our **Lucky Gecko Verbal Reasoning Revision Questions** (Book 2), which gently introduces students to the concept of working through questions at an appropriate pace.

In this book, questions are presented in multiple choice format, and all answers should be marked clearly on the answer sheets provided. If your child is taking a multiple choice exam, it is worth noting that answers are often marked by a computer which looks for an appropriate pattern of pencil marks in the boxes provided. For this reason, it is important that they don't show any working out on the answer sheets, and that they mark their answers clearly for each question. Failure to do so may result in the answer being marked incorrect. For the same reason, it is also important that your child gets into the habit of using a pencil, so that they can easily change or erase answers.

According to standard practice for Verbal Reasoning, questions that require two answers must be completely correct to gain the mark - half marks are never awarded.

On each page, we have included a 'Rate This Type' star, which is for the student to colour in either red, orange or green once they have completed the set of questions. This is designed to help the student or parent easily identify the areas of strength and weakness so that further revision can be as focussed as possible.

We hope you find this book useful and we wish your child every success in their exams.

We do more than just Verbal Reasoning... to find out more about our small, friendly tuition company, please visit us at **www.luckygecko.com** .

Our resident geckos are always busily working on new books, so keep checking the website to see our whole collection.

Hello from Lucky Gecko!

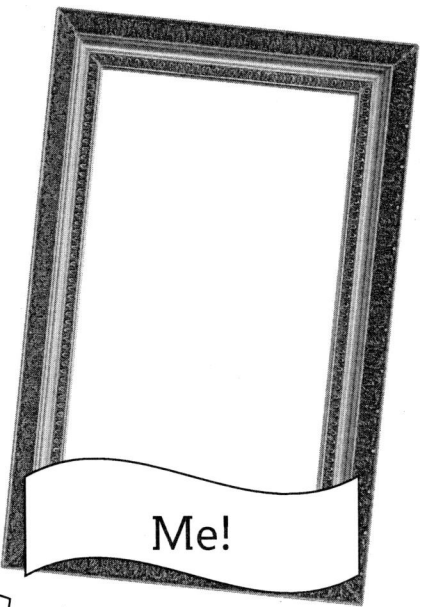

Me!

Welcome to our Verbal Reasoning book. We hope you like it!

Please fill in some information about yourself.

This book belongs to: _____

My school: _____

My favourite subject: _____

My favourite film: _____

Draw a picture of yourself here

Read me!

In this book you will find 21 different types of questions.

We have included a star at the end of each type, which we would like you to colour in. Choose either **red**, **orange** or **green** once you have completed each set of questions to show how you feel about them. Be as honest as you can when picking your colour - it will help you to see where you need to improve.

Here is a guide to help you choose:

	Red	I really didn't like this type. It was one of my least favourites and I found them very tricky.
	Orange	I didn't mind this type too much. It isn't my favourite but I felt I could work through them fairly confidently.
	Green	I really liked this type! It is one of my favourites and I felt happy and confident doing all of the questions.

Remember...

Some really helpful tips

* Make sure you mark your answers clearly and don't do <u>**ANY**</u> working out on the answer sheet - it's for answers only!

* Be careful to **MARK THE RIGHT NUMBER OF ANSWERS** down for each question. Some questions only need one answer, while others need two. If you put down the wrong number, you'll lose the mark.

* <u>**DON'T PANIC!!**</u> If you start to feel stressed, take a deep breath and do your best to relax. You can't concentrate properly if you're worrying!

Letter Sequences

Find the next two letters in each sequence and mark them on the answer sheet. The alphabet has been provided to help you.

A B C D E F G H I J K L M N O P Q R S T U V W X Y Z

For example: AC   BD   CE   DF   EG   **FH**

1. KD, LE, MF, NG, OH
2. TX, SY, RZ, QA, PB
3. DF, FE, HD, JC, LB
4. AP, DR, GT, JV, MX
5. DF, XL, RR, LX, FD
6. IF, HD, JE, IC, KD, JB, LC
7. KV, OY, SB, WE, AH
8. LC, OF, SJ, XO, DU
9. CB, EZ, GX, IV, KT, MR
10. LP, RO, XN, DM, JL
11. SK, SH, PH, PE, ME, MB, JB
12. AI, DF, GC, JZ, MW, PT
13. WL, YN, AP, CR, ET
14. TB, QY, MU, JR, FN, CK
15. EC, GF, OI, QL, YO, AR
16. DH, CL, BP, AT, ZX, YB
17. CC, HX, MS, RN, WI
18. LW, OA, RE, UI, XM
19. JE, IF, HG, GH, FI, EJ
20. VR, PV, JZ, DD, XH, RL
21. XP, VN, SK, OG, JB
22. NJ, WH, FF, OD, XB, GZ
23. MA, QD, UG, YJ, CM, GP
24. OY, IA, CC, WE, QG
25. PE, UJ, AP, FU, LA, QF
26. SQ, OM, VT, RP, YW, US, BZ

Your colour rating....

Question 1	
LK	
PI	
OJ	
PH	
QI	

Question 2	
NC	
OC	
NZ	
MB	
OD	

Question 3	
MB	
LC	
NA	
PZ	
AM	

Question 4	
PZ	
OY	
NZ	
PA	
QW	

Question 5	
YK	
JA	
ZJ	
XL	
RO	

Question 6	
LZ	
KY	
GD	
KA	
HW	

Question 7	
FL	
DP	
FO	
EK	
DL	

Question 8	
KB	
MY	
HA	
LZ	
GC	

Question 9	
OQ	
OR	
OO	
OL	
OP	

Question 10	
PM	
KR	
NO	
PK	
MP	

Question 11	
KZ	
RV	
TX	
MA	
JY	

Question 12	
RQ	
SP	
RS	
SQ	
RR	

Question 13	
HW	
GV	
CX	
GY	
DA	

Question 14	
FH	
ZH	
YG	
YK	
RD	

Question 15	
IU	
DU	
IX	
CO	
DW	

Question 16	
XE	
XL	
XR	
XC	
XF	

Question 17	
SN	
RM	
BD	
AC	
BE	

Question 18	
AP	
YP	
ZR	
AQ	
ZQ	

Question 19	
FI	
DK	
FK	
DI	
EJ	

Question 20	
LP	
SN	
LQ	
KP	
SO	

Question 21	
EW	
JB	
EU	
DV	
KV	

Question 22	
PA	
NW	
PX	
OY	
PV	

Question 23	
JR	
LQ	
KS	
KR	
LT	

Question 24	
HI	
LL	
HK	
MJ	
KI	

Question 25	
XL	
WL	
YK	
ZG	
VR	

Question 26	
WU	
XV	
WW	
YU	
ZV	

Your score....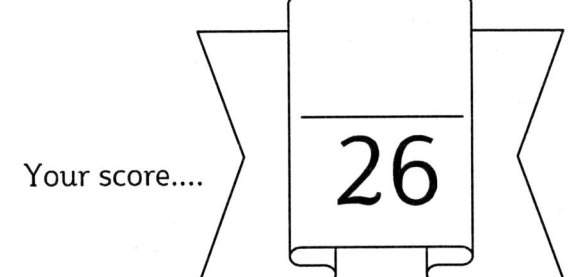

Letter Analogies

In each question below, find the two letters that will best complete the sentence and mark them on the answer sheet. The alphabet has been provided to help you.

A B C D E F G H I J K L M N O P Q R S T U V W X Y Z

For example: AC is to BD, as CI is to **DJ**

1.   JN is to KM, as RV is to _____
2.   FL is to EJ, as CX is to _____
3.   ZD is to BH, as YK is to _____
4.   AQ is to YS, as PT is to _____
5.   TG is to SI, as RH is to _____
6.   IM is to EP, as TF is to _____
7.   CB is to ZD, as SD is to _____
8.   HB is to LX, as MW is to _____
9.   OJ is to RO, as UY is to _____
10. ZA is to YY, as LI is to _____
11. EX is to GA, as QU is to _____
12. BE is to YV, as DI is to _____
13. HZ is to JY, as ML is to _____
14. CC is to FG, as DJ is to _____
15. LC is to JZ, as EA is to _____
16. FH is to KK, as WW is to _____
17. YA is to WZ, as NU is to _____
18. DE is to HG, as PQ is to _____
19. OI is to OH, as XO is to _____
20. VY is to TB, as HH is to _____
21. ZK is to AP, as YT is to _____
22. MM is to NO, as NH is to _____
23. XZ is to BW, as YG is to _____
24. IP is to KS, as UF is to _____
25. EE is to BH, as DL is to _____
26. YJ is to DG, as ZO is to _____

Your colour rating....

Question 1		Question 2		Question 3		Question 4		Question 5		Question 6	
RU	☐	AV	☐	AO	☐	OR	☐	PI	☐	PK	☐
SU	☐	ZA	☐	CP	☐	NV	☐	NH	☐	LG	☐
SV	☐	BX	☐	BI	☐	VN	☐	QJ	☐	PI	☐
QP	☐	BV	☐	BL	☐	NW	☐	PJ	☐	HJ	☐
WV	☐	AW	☐	ZN	☐	MV	☐	LM	☐	FD	☐

Question 7		Question 8		Question 9		Question 10		Question 11		Question 12	
MG	☐	RT	☐	ZB	☐	GA	☐	RX	☐	ZY	☐
PA	☐	QS	☐	SL	☐	PO	☐	ST	☐	WR	☐
PD	☐	RS	☐	XD	☐	KK	☐	RL	☐	VA	☐
MK	☐	SL	☐	CX	☐	JI	☐	SX	☐	WI	☐
PF	☐	TP	☐	XB	☐	KG	☐	SW	☐	RA	☐

Question 13		Question 14		Question 15		Question 16		Question 17		Question 18	
TP	☐	GN	☐	CZ	☐	CD	☐	JT	☐	TS	☐
RC	☐	FF	☐	BX	☐	BZ	☐	NV	☐	RT	☐
VA	☐	KL	☐	AD	☐	FZ	☐	LT	☐	RR	☐
OK	☐	GS	☐	LV	☐	YU	☐	IV	☐	TT	☐
RA	☐	QK	☐	CX	☐	BY	☐	LU	☐	RS	☐

Question 19		Question 20		Question 21		Question 22		Question 23		Question 24	
XM	☐	GK	☐	XT	☐	MK	☐	BC	☐	WI	☐
NX	☐	DJ	☐	VQ	☐	OK	☐	CD	☐	VK	☐
XL	☐	IL	☐	XP	☐	OJ	☐	BD	☐	UL	☐
XN	☐	EJ	☐	VW	☐	PR	☐	CA	☐	UJ	☐
MY	☐	FK	☐	BG	☐	MP	☐	AE	☐	VP	☐

Question 25		Question 26	
ZP	☐	EL	☐
YR	☐	DO	☐
AO	☐	FN	☐
BM	☐	DM	☐
AN	☐	EN	☐

Your score....

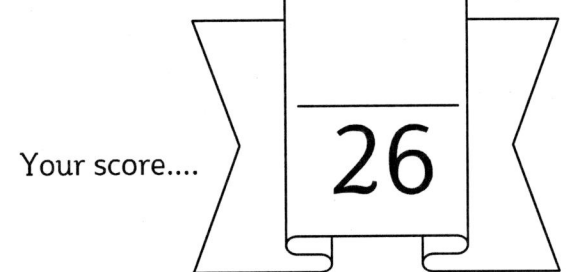

Code Words

In each of the following questions, words have been written in code. You must work out the word o code which will complete the sentence and mark it on the answer sheet provided. The alphabet has been given to help you.

A B C D E F G H I J K L M N O P Q R S T U V W X Y Z

For example: If the code for KIND is LJOE,
what is the code for TYPE?   **UZQF**

1. If the code for WATCH is AEXGL what is the code for CLOCK?

2. If the code for SMELL is MGYFF what is the code for SIGHT?

3. If the code for OFFICE is RIILFH what is the code for STUDY?

4. If BFXYJ means WASTE what does GNS mean?

5. If the code for HORSE is IQUWJ what is the code for SHEEP?

6. If the code for MOVIE is OMXGG what does EGPCOY mean?

7. If WHEAJ means ALIEN what does IWCEY mean?

8. If BQQWO means THING what is the code for DREAM?

9. If NYRPMJ means PATROL what is the code for BEHIND?

10. If the code for CRIME is XIRNV what is the code for COVER?

11. If KMSAGS means LOVELY what does BFXJXY mean?

12. If the code for SPELL is VOHKO what does IHURW mean?

13. If the code for ASLEEP is ZHOVVK what is the code for POSTER?

14. If the code for FRYING is YKRBGZ what is the code for FORGIVE?

15. If ASVVC means WORRY what is the code for TRUTH?

16. If KTXXH means HOUSE what does DQZFBX mean?

Question 1		Question 2		Question 3		Question 4		Question 5		Question 6	
FPSRO	☐	YOMJR	☐	VVYGB	☐	CAN	☐	SIGGT	☐	GROUND	☐
HPLMA	☐	MCABN	☐	VWXGB	☐	ALL	☐	RGBAN	☐	CERISE	☐
GQTGO	☐	NDFIU	☐	WTXRA	☐	BAN	☐	TJHIV	☐	CINEMA	☐
GPSGO	☐	MDABM	☐	PQRGC	☐	BIN	☐	TGGHS	☐	GIRAFFE	☐
YHKTM	☐	LKGZT	☐	TLKPR	☐	LAX	☐	TJHIU	☐	CINDER	☐

Question 7		Question 8		Question 9		Question 10		Question 11		Question 12	
EARTH	☐	LAMJU	☐	YCFGLD	☐	WOEVJ	☐	CHANCE	☐	LEMON	☐
MAGIC	☐	MZLHU	☐	ZBRPWT	☐	XLEUI	☐	DIARY	☐	FIRST	☐
MAIDS	☐	LZMJV	☐	YBFFNA	☐	WLEWK	☐	CHANGE	☐	LIVER	☐
EIDER	☐	LAMKU	☐	ZCFGLB	☐	XNEVI	☐	CIRCLE	☐	FIRED	☐
MOUTH	☐	LXDVR	☐	ZCFHLB	☐	XLEVI	☐	BEWARE	☐	FRIED	☐

Question 13		Question 14		Question 15		Question 16	
KLHGVI	☐	YGLZBNX	☐	PNTWD	☐	ALWAYS	☐
KLGHVI	☐	ZGKZBOY	☐	XVYLX	☐	GAMMON	☐
ONRQFS	☐	YHKZBOX	☐	PLRVA	☐	GALLOP	☐
JLHHUI	☐	MVYKPAL	☐	XVYXL	☐	APPEAR	☐
KLHFUI	☐	YHZKBOX	☐	XRUXL	☐	AROMAS	☐

Keep going.... There's more over the page!

A B C D E F G H I J K L M N O P Q R S T U V W X Y Z

17. If the code for RESULT is LYMOFN what does MOGGYL mean?

18. If the code for WINDOW is YGPBQU what is the code for GARAGE?

19. If the code for MUSIC is EMKAU what does SDANW mean?

20. If the code for GLACIER is TOZXRVI what does YVZXS mean?

21. If YMNSP means THINK what is the code for DRINK?

22. If WYRHEC means SUNDAY what does QEVGL mean?

23. If the code for HUMAN is GVLBM what does LPMLDZ mean?

24. If the code for GIVEN is DFSBK what is the code for TAKEN?

25. If the code for LEARN is OIDVQ what is the code for TEACH?

26. If KZIVMG is the code for PARENT what is the code for CHILD?

Your colour rating....

Question 17	Question 18	Question 19	Question 20	Question 21	Question 22
GUARDS ☐	ECSCFH ☐	KIOSK ☐	BEADS ☐	IWNSP ☐	UNTIL ☐
SIMMER ☐	ITYIYC ☐	ALTER ☐	LIVES ☐	YMDWN ☐	MARCH ☐
SUMMER ☐	EYQBIC ☐	BRAIN ☐	LINKS ☐	KLNSP ☐	NEVER ☐
GIBBON ☐	IRVULD ☐	BROWN ☐	BEACH ☐	WINSP ☐	LATER ☐
SHRINE ☐	IYTYIC ☐	ALIVE ☐	BIRDS ☐	WINPS ☐	POINT ☐

Question 23	Question 24	Question 25	Question 26
KIDNEY ☐	VBJFM ☐	WIDKL ☐	XSQOW ☐
MONKEY ☐	WDNDO ☐	XHGBK ☐	HGRDX ☐
NOTICE ☐	QXHBK ☐	XGHAJ ☐	HRGDX ☐
BEING ☐	WDDNO ☐	WIDGK ☐	HHLTV ☐
FRIEND ☐	QXBHK ☐	XHFBK ☐	XSROW ☐

Your score.... / 26

Word Formation

In the following questions there are three pairs of words. You must find the pattern and use it to complete the third pair in the same way as the first two pairs. Find the missing word and mark it on the multiple choice answer sheet.

For example: (spout, out)   (solid, lid)   (depot, **pot**)

1.   (worry, row)   (track, art)   (broad,   )

2.   (world, old)   (table, ale)   (great,   )

3.   (cable, able)   (glass, lass)   (clean,   )

4.   (plate, teal)   (crate, tear)   (drape,   )

5.   (tried, diet)   (stare, ears)   (dream,   )

6.   (tyres, rest)   (shape, apes)   (diner,   )

7.   (grape, gape)   (mouse, muse)   (snail,   )

8.   (water, tear)   (final, nail)   (areas,   )

9.   (drink, rink)   (price, rice)   (space,   )

10. (stamp, ramp)   (trend, send)   (creep,   )

11. (tears, east)   (stomp, tops)   (swing,   )

12. (trace, react)   (shale, heals)   (shire,   )

13. (trees, rest)   (grain, rang)   (spike,   )

14. (cream, cram)   (table, tale)   (clean,   )

Question 1		Question 2		Question 3		Question 4		Question 5		Question 6	
rob	☐	get	☐	lean	☐	read	☐	dame	☐	dine	☐
orb	☐	tag	☐	clan	☐	reap	☐	made	☐	rind	☐
dab	☐	rat	☐	lane	☐	pear	☐	deem	☐	nine	☐
oar	☐	ate	☐	cane	☐	reed	☐	dear	☐	nerd	☐
rod	☐	eat	☐	lace	☐	peer	☐	mead	☐	dire	☐

Question 7		Question 8		Question 9		Question 10		Question 11		Question 12	
sail	☐	rare	☐	aces	☐	sleep	☐	wigs	☐	heirs	☐
salt	☐	earl	☐	pace	☐	cape	☐	wing	☐	hire	☐
nail	☐	rest	☐	apes	☐	beep	☐	sing	☐	rise	☐
ails	☐	ears	☐	peas	☐	reap	☐	swig	☐	hers	☐
snap	☐	seas	☐	seep	☐	greed	☐	wins	☐	sire	☐

Question 13		Question 14	
pike	☐	near	☐
keep	☐	lane	☐
pies	☐	lean	☐
peek	☐	clan	☐
pick	☐	cane	☐

Keep going.... There's more over the page!

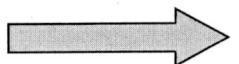

15. (fleas, leaf)　(trend, rent)　(soars,　　)

16. (sorry, rosy)　(balls, labs)　(trams,　　)

17. (glass, sags)　(shirk, risk)　(shift,　　)

18. (girls, rigs)　(brows, orbs)　(crash,　　)

19. (smile, miles)　(score, cores)　(share,　　)

20. (flame, game)　(blame, came)　(knock,　　)

21. (snare, near)　(shade, head)　(frame,　　)

22. (flame, leaf)　(stare, teas)　(plate,　　)

23. (eider, ride)　(cores, sore)　(cover,　　)

24. (store, toes)　(shift, hits)　(train,　　)

25. (aside, said)　(alter, late)　(asked,　　)

26. (regal, gale)　(ashen, hens)　(feels,　　)

Your colour rating....

Question 15	
soar	☐
roar	☐
rose	☐
sore	☐
oars	☐

Question 16	
rams	☐
arms	☐
arts	☐
star	☐
mass	☐

Question 17	
this	☐
fish	☐
fits	☐
hits	☐
fist	☐

Question 18	
arch	☐
char	☐
rash	☐
asks	☐
scar	☐

Question 19	
hears	☐
sheer	☐
areas	☐
heals	☐
hares	☐

Question 20	
rock	☐
lock	☐
sock	☐
block	☐
flock	☐

Question 21	
ream	☐
fear	☐
reef	☐
mare	☐
free	☐

Question 22	
pate	☐
late	☐
peat	☐
leap	☐
teal	☐

Question 23	
cove	☐
over	☐
rove	☐
ever	☐
race	☐

Question 24	
rail	☐
ants	☐
into	☐
rant	☐
rain	☐

Question 25	
sake	☐
dash	☐
seed	☐
seek	☐
desk	☐

Question 26	
self	☐
less	☐
else	☐
eels	☐
feel	☐

Your score.... 26

Word Formation 2

In each of the following questions, the word in brackets is made using letters taken from the word outside the brackets. You must find the pattern for the first group of words and use it to complete the missing word from the second group in the same way. Find the missing word and mark it on the multiple choice answer sheet.

For example: night   (hate)   maple

comma   (**meal**)   peril

1. track   [tale]   below
   paint   [   ]   bells

2. think   [than]   great
   seals   [   ]   treat

3. catch   [itch]   flies
   slice   [   ]   sunny

4. shoes   [sock]   clock
   cloud   [   ]   stall

5. tried   [darts]   start
   rains   [   ]   score

6. drain   [raid]   flare
   sails   [   ]   sheep

7. hover   [oven]   stone
   blink   [   ]   thief

8. stake   [meat]   prism
   slate   [   ]   spied

9. maker   [peak]   paste
   arrow   [   ]   husky

10. horse   [close]   climb
    sever   [   ]   stand

11. moles   [pane]   plane
    swaps   [   ]   snail

12. trace   [feat]   flint
    clear   [   ]   table

13. polar   [real]   dream
    totem   [   ]   croak

14. locks   [sale]   beads
    goats   [   ]   snide

15. sport   [port]   phone
    shine   [   ]   moans

16. joker   [meek]   rhyme
    madam   [   ]   ladle

17. prize   [ship]   stash
    areas   [   ]   petal

18. dwarf   [ward]   sword
    gloat   [   ]   dryer

Question 1		Question 2		Question 3		Question 4		Question 5		Question 6	
pill	☐	rest	☐	nice	☐	dots	☐	saint	☐	ease	☐
pile	☐	eats	☐	lies	☐	tall	☐	cores	☐	eels	☐
pant	☐	last	☐	cell	☐	clot	☐	roars	☐	lies	☐
bile	☐	teal	☐	less	☐	loud	☐	soars	☐	sail	☐
leap	☐	tree	☐	nuns	☐	call	☐	snare	☐	peel	☐

Question 7		Question 8		Question 9		Question 10		Question 11		Question 12	
life	☐	pies	☐	rows	☐	sands	☐	snap	☐	real	☐
file	☐	tale	☐	hour	☐	verse	☐	wasp	☐	race	☐
link	☐	deal	☐	husk	☐	saves	☐	sail	☐	blue	☐
thin	☐	dies	☐	asks	☐	steer	☐	slap	☐	tale	☐
tent	☐	slap	☐	wash	☐	vends	☐	nail	☐	tree	☐

Question 13		Question 14		Question 15		Question 16		Question 17		Question 18	
coat	☐	tide	☐	hone	☐	lead	☐	tale	☐	load	☐
meat	☐	sign	☐	main	☐	made	☐	sale	☐	roar	☐
moat	☐	oats	☐	home	☐	deal	☐	peal	☐	gory	☐
team	☐	gnat	☐	mane	☐	male	☐	peel	☐	road	☐
take	☐	side	☐	mean	☐	lame	☐	plea	☐	tell	☐

Keep going.... There's more over the page!

19. lions   [mile]   slime

    circle   [   ]   handed

20. eagle   [east]   storm

    talon   [   ]   meant

21. spoon   [ants]   state

    drake   [   ]   fable

22. glove   [veal]   rival

    shape   [   ]   first

23. great   [true]   plume

    stops   [   ]   scary

24. watch   [chat]   grate

    pulse   [   ]   plain

25. float   [loaf]   jolly

    evils   [   ]   fires

26. devil   [lead]   scale

    sheep   [   ]   steal

Your colour rating....

Question 19	
dice	☐
land	☐
rice	☐
deed	☐
clan	☐

Question 20	
team	☐
mate	☐
late	☐
name	☐
loan	☐

Question 21	
bled	☐
read	☐
bead	☐
leaf	☐
real	☐

Question 22	
rips	☐
past	☐
pear	☐
spit	☐
pest	☐

Question 23	
pots	☐
stay	☐
taps	☐
scar	☐
spot	☐

Question 24	
pain	☐
sail	☐
nail	☐
seal	☐
leap	☐

Question 25	
rile	☐
sire	☐
reef	☐
file	☐
view	☐

Question 26	
ales	☐
step	☐
peas	☐
eats	☐
also	☐

Your score.... 26

Code Matching

In each of the questions below, there are four words and three codes. Each code matches one of the words, but they are not written in the right order. One of the words does not have a code. Work out the correct code for each word and then answer the questions that follow. Mark your answer on the multiple choice answer sheet provided.

TREE   RATS   EATS   SCAR

8743   6322   3468

1. What is the code for TREATS?
2. What is the code for CARTS?
3. What does 63472 mean?

HOLE   LEAF   FEEL   HALO

3157   5218   3752

4. What does 8715 mean?
5. What is the code for HEEL?
6. What does 5718 mean?

KITE   ITEM   MALE   TOUT

1352   4784   6421

7. What is the code for MULLET?
8. What does 1342 mean?
9. What is the code for TALE?

DAYS   FEAR   FARM   MEAD

4285   5726   6213

10. What is the code for MADE?
11. What does 57881 mean?
12. What does 48257 mean?

DRUM   LURK   MEND   RAIL

1237   6324   4596

13. What does 426615 mean?
14. What is the code for MEEK?
15. What does 3215 mean?

NAME   MILD   MILE   MEAL

4628   9246   4581

16. What does 966186 mean?
17. What does 8546 mean?
18. What is the code for ENAMEL?

Question 1	
623468	☐
632486	☐
643286	☐
632468	☐
634268	☐

Question 2	
86743	☐
74368	☐
23687	☐
73486	☐
73468	☐

Question 3	
RACES	☐
RATES	☐
STARE	☐
TARTS	☐
TRACE	☐

Question 4	
FOAL	☐
FALL	☐
HEAL	☐
FOOL	☐
HALE	☐

Question 5	
5332	☐
2557	☐
3225	☐
2325	☐
8225	☐

Question 6	
HALL	☐
HALF	☐
LOAF	☐
HALE	☐
LOVE	☐

Question 7	
185542	☐
182251	☐
814462	☐
816652	☐
185524	☐

Question 8	
TAME	☐
MATE	☐
LOUT	☐
MOAT	☐
LIKE	☐

Question 9	
6784	☐
6354	☐
4352	☐
6754	☐
4532	☐

Question 10	
6726	☐
5267	☐
6275	☐
5627	☐
5726	☐

Question 11	
FERRY	☐
MERRY	☐
MARRY	☐
FREES	☐
SMEAR	☐

Question 12	
DREAM	☐
REAMS	☐
FRAYS	☐
REEFS	☐
FRAME	☐

Question 13	
MUDDLE	☐
KINDLE	☐
MEDDLE	☐
MURDER	☐
DIMMER	☐

Question 14	
5447	☐
4557	☐
2443	☐
6229	☐
4773	☐

Question 15	
RULE	☐
MINE	☐
LEND	☐
RILE	☐
RUDE	☐

Question 16	
NAILED	☐
MILDEW	☐
MAILED	☐
AMBLED	☐
NEEDLE	☐

Question 17	
MAIL	☐
LEAD	☐
DEEM	☐
DEAL	☐
LIME	☐

Question 18	
956824	☐
965428	☐
692468	☐
698264	☐
694268	☐

Keep going.... There's more over the page!

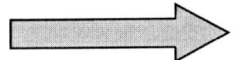

DUCK   LACE   YEAR   RAKE

4351   2759   6138

19. What is the code for LUCKY?

20. What does 28391 mean?

21. What does 813446 mean?

ROAM   MAST   CLIP   CLAP

8762   4531   8732

22. What is the code for RAIL?

23. What does 2431 mean?

24. What does 7634 mean?

REEF   DIAL   PAID   PORE

2465   3817   3642

25. What is the code for LADLE?

26. What does 21762 mean?

27. What is the code for PADDLE?

Question 19	
47569	☐
23591	☐
47596	☐
25391	☐
15391	☐

Question 20	
RACER	☐
DRAKE	☐
EARLY	☐
RAKED	☐
DUKES	☐

Question 21	
YEARLY	☐
CREAKY	☐
CREASE	☐
REALLY	☐
CRACKS	☐

Question 22	
4367	☐
4673	☐
8632	☐
4637	☐
8367	☐

Question 23	
RAIN	☐
CLAM	☐
ROAM	☐
MOAT	☐
PRAM	☐

Question 24	
ARMS	☐
LAIR	☐
OPAL	☐
LIAR	☐
LIPS	☐

Question 25	
65237	☐
56257	☐
73475	☐
56527	☐
56275	☐

Question 26	
PRIDE	☐
DRILL	☐
LAPEL	☐
DREAD	☐
DRAPE	☐

Question 27	
362257	☐
426618	☐
632275	☐
367721	☐
632257	☐

Your score.... 27

Missing Letters

In each of the questions below, find one letter that will complete the word in front of the brackets, and begin the word after the brackets. The same letter must fit into both sets of brackets. Mark your answer on the multiple choice answer sheet provided.

For example: CA (**T**) ALK   FLA (**T**) ALL

1. FOO (T) HEY, CAR (T) RICK
2. DOO (R) OOM, SHOWE (R) ICH
3. BAT (H) OSE, CATC (H) OLD
4. SLU (M) UCH, BOO (M) ONEY
5. SHEL (L) EAVE, HIL (L) EAN
6. FLAS (K) ING, TAL (K) IND
7. BRIN (G) REET, SLU (G) ONE
8. HEA (P) LOT, KEE (P) ANIC
9. WHIS (K) ITE, SLEE (K) IND
10. LEA (F) OAL, CLIF (F) EVER
11. STE (W) ATER, BLO (W) IDOW
12. PAT (H) OLES, WRAT (H) IDE
13. SPI (T) OIL, DAR (T) OLD
14. SLOP (E) ARLY, SID (E) AGER
15. BOL (T) IDY, EDI (T) ONE
16. SKI (D) RAB, MEN (D) RIVE
17. MIS (S) EVER, SIGH (S) HOCK
18. SMU (G) EAR, BEIN (G) OAT
19. HU (B) EAK, CLU (B) RINK
20. DEN (Y) EAR, PENN (Y) ELP
21. SLIC (E) ACH, WAST (E) NTER
22. ALAR (M) OST, CAL (M) INCE
23. SLOT (H) OPE, LAUG (H) ERE
24. ROT (A) NGER, QUOT (A) LOOF
25. JOIN (T) AKES, LOO (T) ENOR
26. LAM (B) UOY, NUM (B) RINE

Your colour rating....

Question 1		Question 2		Question 3		Question 4		Question 5		Question 6	
L	☐	R	☐	H	☐	G	☐	F	☐	H	☐
T	☐	M	☐	S	☐	K	☐	M	☐	T	☐
R	☐	L	☐	B	☐	M	☐	T	☐	K	☐
D	☐	T	☐	D	☐	H	☐	K	☐	I	☐
S	☐	D	☐	E	☐	T	☐	L	☐	Y	☐

Question 7		Question 8		Question 9		Question 10		Question 11		Question 12	
K	☐	T	☐	T	☐	F	☐	M	☐	E	☐
D	☐	P	☐	P	☐	G	☐	B	☐	W	☐
W	☐	F	☐	K	☐	N	☐	L	☐	H	☐
G	☐	R	☐	W	☐	V	☐	G	☐	L	☐
C	☐	L	☐	M	☐	D	☐	W	☐	N	☐

Question 13		Question 14		Question 15		Question 16		Question 17		Question 18	
L	☐	W	☐	F	☐	S	☐	T	☐	G	☐
G	☐	Y	☐	C	☐	T	☐	S	☐	T	☐
N	☐	N	☐	T	☐	C	☐	L	☐	C	☐
T	☐	E	☐	R	☐	D	☐	W	☐	D	☐
E	☐	S	☐	E	☐	P	☐	B	☐	M	☐

Question 19		Question 20		Question 21		Question 22		Question 23		Question 24	
D	☐	T	☐	K	☐	C	☐	N	☐	A	☐
B	☐	H	☐	E	☐	F	☐	L	☐	E	☐
L	☐	W	☐	I	☐	W	☐	S	☐	S	☐
E	☐	Y	☐	H	☐	T	☐	H	☐	U	☐
P	☐	J	☐	T	☐	M	☐	E	☐	O	☐

Question 25		Question 26	
M	☐	E	☐
S	☐	G	☐
T	☐	T	☐
K	☐	B	☐
C	☐	F	☐

Your score....

Hidden Words

In each of the sentences below there is a four letter word which has been hidden at the end of one word and the beginning of the next. Find the pair of words that contain the hidden word and mark it on the answer sheet.

For example: They played the ga**me at** home. = **meat**

1. They ate until everything was gone.

2. Is that ripe enough to eat?

3. Dave just bought a new stereo.

4. What if the bus is late?

5. That wine is for special occasions.

6. Look what Tom bought for us!

7. Our new hens are laying well.

8. Work a little bit every day.

9. We left the car down there.

10. Sarah and Jane have gone out.

11. We will order the food later.

12. I do homework after my dinner.

13. The irises grow very well here.

14. The thief tried everything to escape.

15. The taxis leave from the station.

16. Peter opened the locked door quietly.

17. My students always ask impossible things!

18. Bravely, the hero began the fight.

19. The town makes money through industry.

20. We didn't give him any sweets.

Question 1	
They ate	☐
ate until	☐
until everything	☐
everything was	☐
was gone	☐

Question 2	
Is that	☐
that ripe	☐
ripe enough	☐
enough to	☐
to eat	☐

Question 3	
Dave just	☐
just bought	☐
bought a	☐
a new	☐
new stereo	☐

Question 4	
What if	☐
if the	☐
the bus	☐
bus is	☐
is late	☐

Question 5	
That wine	☐
wine is	☐
is for	☐
for special	☐
special occasions	☐

Question 6	
Look what	☐
what Tom	☐
Tom bought	☐
bought for	☐
for us	☐

Question 7	
Our new	☐
new hens	☐
hens are	☐
are laying	☐
laying well	☐

Question 8	
Work a	☐
a little	☐
little bit	☐
bit every	☐
every day	☐

Question 9	
We left	☐
left the	☐
the car	☐
car down	☐
down there	☐

Question 10	
Sarah and	☐
and Jane	☐
Jane have	☐
have gone	☐
gone out	☐

Question 11	
We will	☐
will order	☐
order the	☐
the food	☐
food later	☐

Question 12	
I do	☐
do homework	☐
homework after	☐
after my	☐
my dinner	☐

Question 13	
The irises	☐
irises grow	☐
grow very	☐
very well	☐
well here	☐

Question 14	
The thief	☐
thief tried	☐
tried everything	☐
everything to	☐
to escape	☐

Question 15	
The taxis	☐
taxis leave	☐
leave from	☐
from the	☐
the station	☐

Question 16	
Peter opened	☐
opened the	☐
the locked	☐
locked door	☐
door quietly	☐

Question 17	
My students	☐
students always	☐
always ask	☐
ask impossible	☐
impossible things	☐

Question 18	
Bravely the	☐
the hero	☐
hero began	☐
began the	☐
the fight	☐

Question 19	
The town	☐
town makes	☐
makes money	☐
money through	☐
through industry	☐

Question 20	
We didn't	☐
didn't give	☐
give him	☐
him any	☐
any sweets	☐

Keep going.... There's more over the page!

21. The hospital kiosk sells lovely chocolates.

22. Surely that would be too lucky?!

23. We threw all the decorations away.

24. You are a great team player!

25. Each evening we help cook dinner.

26. That piano seems out of tune.

Your colour rating....

Question 21	
The hospital	☐
hospital kiosk	☐
kiosk sells	☐
sells lovely	☐
lovely chocolates	☐

Question 22	
Surely that	☐
that would	☐
would be	☐
be too	☐
too lucky	☐

Question 23	
We threw	☐
threw all	☐
all the	☐
the decorations	☐
decorations away	☐

Question 24	
You are	☐
are a	☐
a great	☐
great team	☐
team player	☐

Question 25	
Each evening	☐
evening we	☐
we help	☐
help cook	☐
cook dinner	☐

Question 26	
That piano	☐
piano seems	☐
seems out	☐
out of	☐
of tune	☐

Your score.... 26

Transferring letters

In these questions, you must take one letter out of the word on the left and place it into the word on the right, making two new words. You can place the letter between any of the letters in the word on the right, but you can't rearrange the letters. Both new words must be spelled correctly.

When you have found the letter that can be moved, mark it on the answer sheet.

For example: CARD   RAW   (**D**)   CAR   DRAW

1. grows   rains
2. clamp   male
3. bread   dine
4. proud   sage
5. plant   meal
6. reign   host
7. thick   clot
8. mince   hip
9. petal   come
10. clout   loud
11. burgle   anger
12. witch   pith
13. grind   much

14. cheat   nice
15. blank   rush
16. plain   bank
17. avoid   fur
18. their   moor
19. facts   lame
20. greed   out
21. front   pea
22. bream   cad
23. ideal   nose
24. point   cast
25. short   seep
26. flower   able

Your colour rating....

Question 1	
G	☐
R	☐
O	☐
W	☐
S	☐

Question 2	
C	☐
L	☐
A	☐
M	☐
P	☐

Question 3	
B	☐
R	☐
E	☐
A	☐
D	☐

Question 4	
P	☐
R	☐
O	☐
U	☐
D	☐

Question 5	
P	☐
L	☐
A	☐
N	☐
T	☐

Question 6	
R	☐
E	☐
I	☐
G	☐
N	☐

Question 7	
T	☐
H	☐
I	☐
C	☐
K	☐

Question 8	
M	☐
I	☐
N	☐
C	☐
E	☐

Question 9	
P	☐
E	☐
T	☐
A	☐
L	☐

Question 10	
C	☐
L	☐
O	☐
U	☐
T	☐

Question 11	
B	☐
U	☐
R	☐
G	☐
L	☐

Question 12	
W	☐
I	☐
T	☐
C	☐
H	☐

Question 13	
G	☐
R	☐
I	☐
N	☐
D	☐

Question 14	
C	☐
H	☐
E	☐
A	☐
T	☐

Question 15	
B	☐
L	☐
A	☐
N	☐
K	☐

Question 16	
P	☐
L	☐
A	☐
I	☐
N	☐

Question 17	
A	☐
V	☐
O	☐
I	☐
D	☐

Question 18	
T	☐
H	☐
E	☐
I	☐
R	☐

Question 19	
F	☐
A	☐
C	☐
T	☐
S	☐

Question 20	
G	☐
R	☐
E	☐
E	☐
D	☐

Question 21	
F	☐
R	☐
O	☐
N	☐
T	☐

Question 22	
B	☐
R	☐
E	☐
A	☐
M	☐

Question 23	
I	☐
D	☐
E	☐
A	☐
L	☐

Question 24	
P	☐
O	☐
I	☐
N	☐
T	☐

Question 25	
S	☐
H	☐
O	☐
R	☐
T	☐

Question 26	
F	☐
L	☐
O	☐
W	☐
E	☐

Your score.... 26

Odd Ones Out

In these questions, three of the five words are related in some way. Find the **TWO** words that **DO NOT** go with these three and mark them **BOTH** on the answer sheet.

For example: knife   spoon   **plate**   **bowl**   fork

1. author sculptor painting statue artist
2. cherry broccoli nectarine pea damson
3. Japan Africa Sweden Mexico Europe
4. deer cow venison veal beef
5. cube hexagon pentagon triangle cylinder
6. beech beach elm pine stalk
7. vile valiant brave feeble heroic
8. school teacher university lesson college
9. paper pen book pencil crayon
10. happy cheerful smile laugh joyous
11. thick top wide middle broad
12. forgive condemn punish penalise pardon
13. vacant occupied empty full uninhabited
14. path track foot print road
15. sole only soul solitary numerous
16. cousin son father relative nephew
17. lamb piglet sow foal mare
18. mouth speech lecture talk hear
19. similar gather congregate alike converge
20. ill rash spot reckless hasty
21. flower pansy tree daisy foxglove
22. paw sock hoof shoe foot
23. Venus Saturn globe orb sphere
24. yacht catamaran sail canoe lake
25. constable detective criminal thief policeman
26. warehouse mansion cottage office flat

Your colour rating....

Question 1		Question 2		Question 3		Question 4		Question 5		Question 6	
author	☐	cherry	☐	Japan	☐	deer	☐	cube	☐	beech	☐
sculptor	☐	broccoli	☐	Africa	☐	cow	☐	hexagon	☐	beach	☐
painting	☐	nectarine	☐	Sweden	☐	venison	☐	pentagon	☐	elm	☐
statue	☐	pea	☐	Mexico	☐	veal	☐	triangle	☐	pine	☐
artist	☐	damson	☐	Europe	☐	beef	☐	cylinder	☐	stalk	☐

Question 7		Question 8		Question 9		Question 10		Question 11		Question 12	
vile	☐	school	☐	paper	☐	happy	☐	thick	☐	forgive	☐
valiant	☐	teacher	☐	pen	☐	cheerful	☐	top	☐	condemn	☐
brave	☐	university	☐	book	☐	smile	☐	wide	☐	punish	☐
feeble	☐	lesson	☐	pencil	☐	laugh	☐	middle	☐	penalise	☐
heroic	☐	college	☐	crayon	☐	joyous	☐	broad	☐	pardon	☐

Question 13		Question 14		Question 15		Question 16		Question 17		Question 18	
vacant	☐	path	☐	sole	☐	cousin	☐	lamb	☐	mouth	☐
occupied	☐	track	☐	only	☐	son	☐	piglet	☐	speech	☐
empty	☐	foot	☐	soul	☐	father	☐	sow	☐	lecture	☐
full	☐	print	☐	solitary	☐	relative	☐	foal	☐	talk	☐
uninhabited	☐	road	☐	numerous	☐	nephew	☐	mare	☐	hear	☐

Question 19		Question 20		Question 21		Question 22		Question 23		Question 24	
similar	☐	ill	☐	flower	☐	paw	☐	Venus	☐	yacht	☐
gather	☐	rash	☐	pansy	☐	sock	☐	Saturn	☐	catamaran	☐
congregate	☐	spot	☐	tree	☐	hoof	☐	globe	☐	sail	☐
alike	☐	reckless	☐	daisy	☐	shoe	☐	orb	☐	canoe	☐
converge	☐	hasty	☐	foxglove	☐	foot	☐	sphere	☐	lake	☐

Question 25		Question 26	
constable	☐	warehouse	☐
detective	☐	mansion	☐
criminal	☐	cottage	☐
thief	☐	office	☐
policeman	☐	flat	☐

Your score.... 26

Synonyms

In these questions, find **TWO** words, **ONE** from each group, that are **CLOSEST IN MEANING**. Mark **BOTH WORDS** on the answer sheet.

For example: (**angry**   tired   smile)
              (yawn   face   **cross**)

1. (dangerous hurt frightened)
    (wild hazardous animal)

2. (bed cot fatigued)
    (exhausted sheet lazy)

3. (church vicar prayer)
    (priest grave serious)

4. (borrow loan take)
    (lone add lend)

5. (wonder rich thoughtful)
    (frugal considerate pauper)

6. (dinghy opinion chance)
    (dull boat water)

7. (cut severe harm)
    (knife paper grave)

8. (open close shut)
    (near door case)

9. (earth planet country)
    (continent soil solar)

10. (smile happy laugh)
    (sad chuckle funny)

11. (cook oven cookie)
    (hot heat biscuit)

12. (light lamp candle)
    (heavy bright hot)

13. (game puzzle trick)
    (fun riddle play)

14. (plumage bird fly)
    (insect animal feathers)

15. (servant obey kin)
    (comply kind poor)

16. (hide seek divide)
    (split find cherish)

17. (cease permit false)
    (teeth halt real)

18. (hand clap stage)
    (theatre applaud prompt)

19. (fantasy amazing fool)
    (magic trick vibrant)

20. (exist experiment exit)
    (imagine trial enter)

21. (win defeat lose)
    (vanquish vague loose)

Question 1
dangerous	☐	wild	☐
hurt	☐	hazardous	☐
frightened	☐	animal	☐

Question 2
bed	☐	exhausted	☐
cot	☐	sheet	☐
fatigued	☐	lazy	☐

Question 3
church	☐	priest	☐
vicar	☐	grave	☐
prayer	☐	serious	☐

Question 4
borrow	☐	lone	☐
loan	☐	add	☐
take	☐	lend	☐

Question 5
wonder	☐	frugal	☐
rich	☐	considerate	☐
thoughtful	☐	pauper	☐

Question 6
dinghy	☐	dull	☐
opinion	☐	boat	☐
chance	☐	water	☐

Question 7
cut	☐	knife	☐
severe	☐	paper	☐
harm	☐	grave	☐

Question 8
open	☐	near	☐
close	☐	door	☐
shut	☐	case	☐

Question 9
earth	☐	continent	☐
planet	☐	soil	☐
country	☐	solar	☐

Question 10
smile	☐	sad	☐
happy	☐	chuckle	☐
laugh	☐	funny	☐

Question 11
cook	☐	hot	☐
oven	☐	heat	☐
cookie	☐	biscuit	☐

Question 12
light	☐	heavy	☐
lamp	☐	bright	☐
candle	☐	hot	☐

Question 13
game	☐	fun	☐
puzzle	☐	riddle	☐
trick	☐	play	☐

Question 14
plumage	☐	insect	☐
bird	☐	animal	☐
fly	☐	feathers	☐

Question 15
servant	☐	comply	☐
obey	☐	kind	☐
kin	☐	poor	☐

Question 16
hide	☐	split	☐
seek	☐	find	☐
divide	☐	cherish	☐

Question 17
cease	☐	teeth	☐
permit	☐	halt	☐
false	☐	real	☐

Question 18
hand	☐	theatre	☐
clap	☐	applaud	☐
stage	☐	prompt	☐

Question 19
fantasy	☐	magic	☐
amazing	☐	trick	☐
fool	☐	vibrant	☐

Question 20
exist	☐	imagine	☐
experiment	☐	trial	☐
exit	☐	enter	☐

Question 21
win	☐	vanquish	☐
defeat	☐	vague	☐
lose	☐	loose	☐

Keep going.... There's more over the page!

22. (cry broken injured)
    (hurt healthy cast)

23. (sculptor statue author)
    (masterpiece sculpture artist)

24. (consume food dinner)
    (breakfast supper broth)

25. (sight eyes sense)
    (believe vision dream)

26. (half core fruit)
    (centre apple pip)

Your colour rating....

Question 22			
cry	☐	hurt	☐
broken	☐	healthy	☐
injured	☐	cast	☐

Question 23			
sculptor	☐	masterpiece	☐
statue	☐	sculpture	☐
author	☐	artist	☐

Question 24			
consume	☐	breakfast	☐
food	☐	supper	☐
dinner	☐	broth	☐

Question 25			
sight	☐	believe	☐
eyes	☐	vision	☐
sense	☐	dream	☐

Question 26			
half	☐	centre	☐
core	☐	apple	☐
fruit	☐	pip	☐

Your score.... 26

Antonyms

In each question below, find **TWO** words, **ONE** from each set of brackets that are the most **OPPOSITE IN MEANING**. Mark **BOTH WORDS** on the answer sheet.

For example: (black   night   **dark**)
(week   colour   **light**)

1. (most   many   little)
   (calm   few   only)

2. (departure   change   dead)
   (altar   visit   arrival)

3. (hide   maintain   strange)
   (retry   reveal   realistic)

4. (helpful   alert   usually)
   (unsuitable   tired   lean)

5. (loathe   like   lend)
   (happy   love   moan)

6. (hope   coax   kind)
   (despair   decide   depend)

7. (shiny   strong   thin)
   (soft   overview   obese)

8. (deny   permit   refuse)
   (adorn   admire   admit)

9. (break   assemble   assist)
   (respect   dismantle   respond)

10. (down   rise   ask)
    (timid   high   plummet)

11. (coarse   course   cope)
    (rough   smooth   straight)

12. (cowardly   bold   bonded)
    (scarce   brave   brought)

13. (let   forbid   accept)
    (pretend   allow   present)

14. (dear   cheer   darling)
    (inexpensive   deer   dainty)

15. (strength   inquire   stung)
    (small   weakness   meek)

16. (point   sharp   pick)
    (object   blunt   choose)

17. (futile   valuable   keen)
    (worry   worthwhile   old)

18. (entire   empty   second)
    (last   partial   special)

19. (stick   uphold   severe)
    (adhere   answer   abolish)

20. (detest   advance   leap)
    (attempt   retreat   release)

21. (opaque   clear   dark)
    (enhance   transparent   mark)

Question 1			
most	☐	calm	☐
many	☐	few	☐
little	☐	only	☐

Question 2			
departure	☐	altar	☐
change	☐	visit	☐
dead	☐	arrival	☐

Question 3			
hide	☐	retry	☐
maintain	☐	reveal	☐
strange	☐	realistic	☐

Question 4			
helpful	☐	unsuitable	☐
alert	☐	tired	☐
usually	☐	lean	☐

Question 5			
loathe	☐	happy	☐
like	☐	love	☐
lend	☐	moan	☐

Question 6			
hope	☐	despair	☐
coax	☐	decide	☐
kind	☐	depend	☐

Question 7			
shiny	☐	soft	☐
strong	☐	overview	☐
thin	☐	obese	☐

Question 8			
deny	☐	adorn	☐
permit	☐	admire	☐
refuse	☐	admit	☐

Question 9			
break	☐	respect	☐
assemble	☐	dismantle	☐
assist	☐	respond	☐

Question 10			
down	☐	timid	☐
rise	☐	high	☐
ask	☐	plummet	☐

Question 11			
coarse	☐	rough	☐
course	☐	smooth	☐
cope	☐	straight	☐

Question 12			
cowardly	☐	scarce	☐
bold	☐	brave	☐
bonded	☐	brought	☐

Question 13			
let	☐	pretend	☐
forbid	☐	allow	☐
accept	☐	present	☐

Question 14			
dear	☐	inexpensive	☐
cheer	☐	deer	☐
darling	☐	dainty	☐

Question 15			
strength	☐	small	☐
inquire	☐	weakness	☐
stung	☐	meek	☐

Question 16			
point	☐	object	☐
sharp	☐	blunt	☐
pick	☐	choose	☐

Question 17			
futile	☐	worry	☐
valuable	☐	worthwhile	☐
keen	☐	old	☐

Question 18			
entire	☐	last	☐
empty	☐	partial	☐
second	☐	special	☐

Question 19			
stick	☐	adhere	☐
uphold	☐	answer	☐
severe	☐	abolish	☐

Question 20			
detest	☐	attempt	☐
advance	☐	retreat	☐
leap	☐	release	☐

Question 21			
opaque	☐	enhance	☐
clear	☐	transparent	☐
dark	☐	mark	☐

Keep going.... There's more over the page!

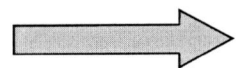

22. (ideal   dredge   deliberate)
    (accidental   loop   think)

23. (reluctant   nocturnal   open)
    (eager   early   spiteful)

24. (scam   scatter   scold)
    (burn   hot   collect)

25. (delight   find   drain)
    (lose   like   loose)

26. (create   minor   flame)
    (rife   destroy   distinguish)

Your colour rating....

Question 22			
ideal	☐	accidental	☐
dredge	☐	loop	☐
deliberate	☐	think	☐

Question 23			
reluctant	☐	eager	☐
nocturnal	☐	early	☐
open	☐	spiteful	☐

Question 24			
scam	☐	burn	☐
scatter	☐	hot	☐
scold	☐	collect	☐

Question 25			
delight	☐	lose	☐
find	☐	like	☐
drain	☐	loose	☐

Question 26			
create	☐	rife	☐
minor	☐	destroy	☐
flame	☐	distinguish	☐

Your score.... 26

Compound Words

In each question below, underline **ONE** word from **BOTH** sets of brackets that together make a new word. The word from the left hand set of brackets always comes first. Mark **BOTH WORDS** on the answer sheet.

For example: (**flower** petal tree)   (bark soft **pot**) = **flowerpot**

1. (star sun light)
   (shine right loop)

2. (table bed picnic)
   (talk crown cloth)

3. (hope like pool)
   (fully cream tide)

4. (mess tidy clean)
   (tie eye age)

5. (fell soap play)
   (told ground post)

6. (am be it)
   (an pit so)

7. (any great buy)
   (day cloak where)

8. (year in goose)
   (lie bent berry)

9. (eat scare knit)
   (crow rely on)

10. (gold car consider)
    (over able low)

11. (cry plea beg)
    (sure aim nut)

12. (tomato jug sauce)
    (take juice pan)

13. (pencil with into)
    (point back draw)

14. (under rope smile)
    (mine stay sing)

15. (open keep over)
    (ink look mist)

16. (work toil mimic)
    (hard to shop)

17. (dart eye mouth)
    (lid move led)

18. (hire man note)
    (kind quick thing)

19. (rat cat malt)
    (him they her)

20. (kid bolt ham)
    (up mock poll)

21. (four for been)
    (team more tune)

Question 1			
star	☐	shine	☐
sun	☐	right	☐
light	☐	loop	☐

Question 2			
table	☐	talk	☐
bed	☐	crown	☐
picnic	☐	cloth	☐

Question 3			
hope	☐	fully	☐
like	☐	cream	☐
pool	☐	tide	☐

Question 4			
mess	☐	tie	☐
tidy	☐	eye	☐
clean	☐	age	☐

Question 5			
fell	☐	told	☐
soap	☐	ground	☐
play	☐	post	☐

Question 6			
am	☐	an	☐
be	☐	pit	☐
it	☐	so	☐

Question 7			
any	☐	day	☐
great	☐	cloak	☐
buy	☐	where	☐

Question 8			
year	☐	lie	☐
in	☐	bent	☐
goose	☐	berry	☐

Question 9			
eat	☐	crow	☐
scare	☐	rely	☐
knit	☐	on	☐

Question 10			
gold	☐	over	☐
car	☐	able	☐
consider	☐	low	☐

Question 11			
cry	☐	sure	☐
plea	☐	aim	☐
beg	☐	nut	☐

Question 12			
tomato	☐	take	☐
jug	☐	juice	☐
sauce	☐	pan	☐

Question 13			
pencil	☐	point	☐
with	☐	back	☐
into	☐	draw	☐

Question 14			
under	☐	mine	☐
rope	☐	stay	☐
smile	☐	sing	☐

Question 15			
open	☐	ink	☐
keep	☐	look	☐
over	☐	mist	☐

Question 16			
work	☐	hard	☐
toil	☐	to	☐
mimic	☐	shop	☐

Question 17			
dart	☐	lid	☐
eye	☐	move	☐
mouth	☐	led	☐

Question 18			
hire	☐	kind	☐
man	☐	quick	☐
note	☐	thing	☐

Question 19			
rat	☐	him	☐
cat	☐	they	☐
malt	☐	her	☐

Question 20			
kid	☐	up	☐
bolt	☐	mock	☐
ham	☐	poll	☐

Question 21			
four	☐	team	☐
for	☐	more	☐
been	☐	tune	☐

Keep going.... There's more over the page!

22. (end   where   so)
    (pace   up   benefit)

23. (in   crane   bother)
    (wrong   hut   finite)

24. (excel   boat   repair)
    (room   wing   led)

25. (went   arrive   go)
    (all   at   did)

26. (learn   know   drink)
    (march   sink   ledge)

Your colour rating....

Question 22			
end	☐	pace	☐
where	☐	up	☐
so	☐	benefit	☐

Question 23			
in	☐	wrong	☐
crane	☐	hut	☐
bother	☐	finite	☐

Question 24			
excel	☐	room	☐
boat	☐	wing	☐
repair	☐	led	☐

Question 25			
went	☐	all	☐
arrive	☐	at	☐
go	☐	did	☐

Question 26			
learn	☐	march	☐
know	☐	sink	☐
drink	☐	ledge	☐

Your score.... 26

Complete the Word

The sentences below all have one word (in capitals) which has had three consecutive letters taken out. The three letters will make a correctly spelled word without changing the order. Find the three letter word which would complete the word in capitals and mark it on the answer sheet.

For example: The toolbox contained a **SNER.** PAN *(SPANNER)*

1. It was so cold that we had to turn the HING up.
2. The shop carried a huge GE of clothes
3. England is in the NORTN hemisphere.
4. Unfortunately, many workers were made UNDANT
5. The boxer was pronounced heavyweight CHION
6. The game kept him OCIED for hours.
7. Parliament DEED the point for many days.
8. The presents were wrapped and tied with beautiful BON
9. The ICIAL score was 2:1.
10. Don't speak to me in that NER.
11. I think I'll wear my favourite TRORS tonight.
12. Where are you thinking of HANG that painting?
13. In the modern world there are many methods of COMMUNIING
14. You must approach these questions in a ICAL way.
15. Would you like SOHING to eat?
16. I think he's the best PER in the team.
17. The public TSPORT around the city was great
18. The CAIN ordered everyone into the lifeboats
19. The footballer had a big ARENT with the referee.
20. It's best to be organised and put everything into a FER.
21. To stay healthy, it's important to be IVE.
22. Those curtains are not to my LIG.
23. My cat keeps SCCHING the sofa!
24. He was given the award in RENITION of all his hard work.
25. The LLORD collects the rent on Thursdays.
26. You can't do that - it's CHING!

Your colour rating....

Question 1		Question 2		Question 3		Question 4		Question 5		Question 6	
EAT	☐	ROW	☐	HIM	☐	URN	☐	WAR	☐	CUB	☐
ATE	☐	TOO	☐	HIS	☐	RED	☐	RAW	☐	YOU	☐
NOT	☐	CAN	☐	HER	☐	HEN	☐	APT	☐	OUT	☐
ROT	☐	RAN	☐	OUR	☐	PAD	☐	AMP	☐	YEW	☐
AND	☐	COP	☐	ERR	☐	PAN	☐	EGG	☐	CUP	☐

Question 7		Question 8		Question 9		Question 10		Question 11		Question 12	
BAT	☐	APE	☐	RAT	☐	TOR	☐	OWE	☐	ONE	☐
BET	☐	RIB	☐	OFF	☐	MEN	☐	RAY	☐	NOT	☐
SEA	☐	RAP	☐	ILL	☐	COT	☐	USE	☐	GIN	☐
BAR	☐	ONE	☐	CAP	☐	MAN	☐	TOP	☐	SHE	☐
SET	☐	ORE	☐	OLD	☐	TAR	☐	SEW	☐	DOE	☐

Question 13		Question 14		Question 15		Question 16		Question 17		Question 18	
TIN	☐	MIT	☐	MET	☐	HOT	☐	RAN	☐	ATE	☐
CAT	☐	RAG	☐	ACE	☐	LAY	☐	FOE	☐	APT	☐
LET	☐	HIS	☐	SKY	☐	BED	☐	ANT	☐	STY	☐
LIT	☐	ELM	☐	CAR	☐	SOW	☐	FOR	☐	TEA	☐
PIT	☐	LOG	☐	WAS	☐	RAY	☐	TEE	☐	LAP	☐

Question 19		Question 20		Question 21		Question 22		Question 23		Question 24	
PEW	☐	OIL	☐	CRY	☐	NOT	☐	RAW	☐	GIG	☐
GUM	☐	AIL	☐	LOT	☐	KIN	☐	ARE	☐	CON	☐
EAR	☐	FAT	☐	ODE	☐	HIT	☐	LAW	☐	COG	☐
DYE	☐	OLD	☐	POT	☐	TEN	☐	RAT	☐	BIG	☐
HAY	☐	OFF	☐	ACT	☐	TIN	☐	ALE	☐	WIT	☐

Question 25		Question 26	
END	☐	ROW	☐
ACE	☐	EAT	☐
AIL	☐	EEL	☐
AND	☐	FIN	☐
ALL	☐	NOR	☐

Your score.... 26

Homonyms

In each question below, there are two pairs of words. By looking at the multiple choice answer sheet, find the word that would go equally well with **BOTH** pairs and mark down your choice.

For example: (dance, party)   (globe, sphere) = **BALL**

1.   (cage, enclosure) (pencil, ballpoint)
2.   (well, OK) (penalty, punishment)
3.   (supporter, enthusiast) (ventilate, blow)
4.   (vault, coffer) (secure, unharmed)
5.   (able, allowed) (jar, tin)
6.   (cope, manage) (lever, grip)
7.   (finger, hand) (oak, ash)
8.   (edge, slope) (fund, treasury)
9.   (sightless, unseeing) (curtain, screen)
10. (park, common) (emerald, lime)
11. (path, trail) (pursue, follow)
12. (correct, accurate) (moral, fair)
13. (hoop, band) (peal, chime)
14. (clock, timepiece) (examine, observe)
15. (adhere, join) (twig, cane)
16. (gap, distance) (universe, cosmos)
17. (field, ground) (throw, fling)
18. (overtake, exceed) (qualify, succeed)
19. (sow, dig) (flower, shrub)
20. (block, jam) (shoe, sandal)
21. (timber, lumber) (forest, copse)
22. (toe, sole) (yard, inch)
23. (ground, terrain) (alight, arrive)
24. (accept, tolerate) (polar, grizzly)
25. (prepare, coach) (engine, locomotive)
26. (plank, panel) (embark, enter)

Your colour rating....

Question 1		Question 2		Question 3		Question 4		Question 5		Question 6	
cell	☐	fine	☐	hit	☐	bank	☐	can	☐	charge	☐
ruler	☐	good	☐	fan	☐	key	☐	permit	☐	push	☐
zoo	☐	charge	☐	breathe	☐	safe	☐	jam	☐	control	☐
pen	☐	ticket	☐	member	☐	lock	☐	box	☐	hold	☐
rubber	☐	great	☐	wind	☐	strong	☐	capable	☐	handle	☐

Question 7		Question 8		Question 9		Question 10		Question 11		Question 12	
tree	☐	money	☐	blind	☐	play	☐	pavement	☐	precise	☐
branch	☐	cliff	☐	deaf	☐	ruby	☐	track	☐	just	☐
nail	☐	bank	☐	carpet	☐	field	☐	chase	☐	right	☐
limb	☐	side	☐	dark	☐	green	☐	lead	☐	change	☐
palm	☐	save	☐	window	☐	lemon	☐	footprint	☐	edit	☐

Question 13		Question 14		Question 15		Question 16		Question 17		Question 18	
skin	☐	test	☐	stick	☐	planet	☐	catch	☐	speed	☐
music	☐	minute	☐	fix	☐	pause	☐	pitch	☐	pass	☐
ring	☐	second	☐	branch	☐	length	☐	grass	☐	win	☐
circle	☐	time	☐	fasten	☐	space	☐	meadow	☐	race	☐
loop	☐	watch	☐	bough	☐	moon	☐	lob	☐	rush	☐

Question 19		Question 20		Question 21		Question 22		Question 23		Question 24	
plant	☐	slipper	☐	carpenter	☐	cod	☐	land	☐	refuse	☐
bush	☐	stop	☐	paper	☐	metre	☐	earth	☐	bear	☐
spade	☐	pause	☐	mill	☐	heart	☐	depart	☐	cold	☐
garden	☐	clog	☐	moss	☐	foot	☐	crush	☐	continent	☐
lawn	☐	stick	☐	wood	☐	garden	☐	soil	☐	drizzle	☐

Question 25		Question 26	
bus	☐	wall	☐
motor	☐	leave	☐
teacher	☐	board	☐
train	☐	door	☐
travel	☐	apply	☐

Your score.... 26

Sentence Analogies

In each of the questions below, find one word from each group that best completes the sentence. Mark **BOTH** words on the multiple choice answer sheet.

For example: Horse is to (race jump **stable**)
                           as bee is to (swarm sky **hive**)

1. Ear is to (head hear chin)
   as eye is to (see lens glasses)

2. Cow is to (calf grass farm)
   as horse is to (ride saddle foal)

3. February is to (December April June)
   as March is to (October May September)

4. Baker is to (loaf dough rise)
   as carpenter is to (wood shop plane)

5. Painting is to (gallery canvas artist)
   as symphony is to (note music composer)

6. Scales are to (fish piano weight)
   as feathers are to (wind wing bird)

7. Tree is to (earth leaf autumn)
   as flower is to (pollen colour petal)

8. Clever is to (correct mark bright)
   as width is to (high breadth volume)

9. Herd is to (sound cattle sheep)
   as pride is to (proud tigers lions)

10. Hour is to (clock minute night)
    as day is to (calendar week sun)

11. Weight is to (stones measure height)
    as distance is to (kilometres length short)

12. Kennel is to (garden dog house)
    as stable is to (hay trough horse)

13. Decade is to (time teen ten)
    as century is to (millennium hundred cricket)

14. Ship is to (boat send dock)
    as aeroplane is to (hangar fly sky)

15. Archery is to (sport arrow aim)
    as tennis is to (racquet court umpire)

16. Mint is to (lamb herb chives)
    as cinnamon is to (spice stick jar)

17. Slip is to (fall envelope slope)
    as jump is to (high gap leap)

18. Green is to (field shade envy)
    as red is to (tired anger link)

19. Pig is to (sty bacon sow)
    as sheep is to (wool mutton flock)

20. Optimist is to (eye hope pessimist)
    as feeble is to (weak strong strength)

21. King is to (queen palace monarch)
    as actor is to (film actress star)

Question 1
head		see	
hear		lens	
chin		glasses	

Question 2
calf		ride	
grass		saddle	
farm		foal	

Question 3
December		October	
April		May	
June		September	

Question 4
loaf		wood	
dough		shop	
rise		plane	

Question 5
gallery		note	
canvas		music	
artist		composer	

Question 6
fish		wind	
piano		wing	
weight		bird	

Question 7
earth		pollen	
leaf		colour	
autumn		petal	

Question 8
correct		high	
mark		breadth	
bright		volume	

Question 9
sound		proud	
cattle		tigers	
sheep		lions	

Question 10
clock		calendar	
minute		week	
night		sun	

Question 11
stones		kilometres	
measure		length	
height		short	

Question 12
garden		hay	
dog		trough	
house		horse	

Question 13
time		millennium	
teen		hundred	
ten		cricket	

Question 14
boat		hangar	
send		fly	
dock		sky	

Question 15
sport		racquet	
arrow		court	
aim		umpire	

Question 16
lamb		spice	
herb		stick	
chives		jar	

Question 17
fall		high	
envelope		gap	
slope		leap	

Question 18
field		tired	
shade		anger	
envy		link	

Question 19
sty		wool	
bacon		mutton	
sow		flock	

Question 20
eye		weak	
hope		strong	
pessimist		strength	

Question 21
queen		film	
palace		actress	
monarch		star	

Keep going.... There's more over the page!

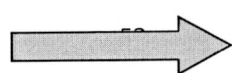

22. Transparent is to (glass clear light)
    as opaque is to (smile clouded object)

23. Sapphire is to (gem jewel blue)
    as emerald is to (green yellow city)

24. Bee is to (hive honey summer)
    as cow is to (rare bull byre)

25. Lone is to (one single loan)
    as pain is to (pane window lock)

26. Finger is to (digit arm hand)
    as toe is to (foot hip shoe)

Your colour rating....

Question 22			
glass	☐	smile	☐
clear	☐	clouded	☐
light	☐	object	☐

Question 23			
gem	☐	green	☐
jewel	☐	yellow	☐
blue	☐	city	☐

Question 24			
hive	☐	rare	☐
honey	☐	bull	☐
summer	☐	byre	☐

Question 25			
one	☐	pane	☐
single	☐	window	☐
loan	☐	lock	☐

Question 26			
digit	☐	foot	☐
arm	☐	hip	☐
hand	☐	shoe	☐

Your score.... 26

Algebra

In each question below, letters stand for numbers. Work out the answer to the sum and mark its **LETTER** on the multiple choice answer sheet.

For example: A = 4, B = 8, C = 2, D = 10, E = 18

   A x C + D = **E**

1. If A = 10, B = 5, C = 2, D = 50, E = 4

    (D - A) ÷ E = _____

2. If A = 8, B = 6, C = 4, D = 3, E = 12

    (A x B) ÷ C = _____

3. If A = 6, B = 14, C = 12, D = 13, E = 2

    B + C - D = _____

4. If A = 100, B = 75, C = 4, D = 50, E = 3

    A ÷ C x E = _____

5. If A = 30, B = 3, C = 7, D = 27, E = 14

    B + D + E - A = ...

6. If A = 15, B = 25, C = 3, D = 5, E = 2

    (A x C + D) ÷ E = _____

7. If A = 10, B = 5, C = 40, D = 200, E = 140

    (D - E - A) ÷ B = _____

8. If A = 12, B = 32, C = 8, D = 20, E = 5

    B ÷ C x E = _____

9. If A = 7, B = 18, C = 5, D = 3, E = 9

    (B ÷ D + E) ÷ C = _____

10. If A = 4, B = 17, C = 8, D = 3, E = 10

    (C x E) ÷ A - D = _____

11. If A = 4, B = 12, C = 13, D = 18, E = 26

    (D + E + A) ÷ B = _____

12. If A = 5, B = 15, C = 1, D = 29, E = 20

    C + D - E + A = _____

13. If A = 36, B = 4, C = 19, D = 14, E = 10

    (C - E) x B = _____

14. If A = 8, B = 7, C = 11, D = 3, E = 13

    (E + A) ÷ D = _____

Question 1	
A	☐
B	☐
C	☐
D	☐
E	☐

Question 2	
A	☐
B	☐
C	☐
D	☐
E	☐

Question 3	
A	☐
B	☐
C	☐
D	☐
E	☐

Question 4	
A	☐
B	☐
C	☐
D	☐
E	☐

Question 5	
A	☐
B	☐
C	☐
D	☐
E	☐

Question 6	
A	☐
B	☐
C	☐
D	☐
E	☐

Question 7	
A	☐
B	☐
C	☐
D	☐
E	☐

Question 8	
A	☐
B	☐
C	☐
D	☐
E	☐

Question 9	
A	☐
B	☐
C	☐
D	☐
E	☐

Question 10	
A	☐
B	☐
C	☐
D	☐
E	☐

Question 11	
A	☐
B	☐
C	☐
D	☐
E	☐

Question 12	
A	☐
B	☐
C	☐
D	☐
E	☐

Question 13	
A	☐
B	☐
C	☐
D	☐
E	☐

Question 14	
A	☐
B	☐
C	☐
D	☐
E	☐

Keep going.... There's more over the page!

15. If A = 10, B = 12, C = 42, D = 9, E = 4

    (C - B) ÷ A x E = _____

16. If A = 9, B = 10, C = 12, D = 7, E = 5

    (D x E + B) ÷ A = _____

17. If A = 4, B = 22, C = 6, D = 24, E = 56

    (A + E - D) ÷ C = _____

18. If A = 40, B = 10, C = 2, D = 34, E = 12

    (D - B) ÷ C = _____

19. If A = 2, B = 17, C = 6, D = 11, E = 14

    (A x D + C) ÷ E = _____

20. If A = 40, B = 75, C = 15, D = 8, E = 20

    B - C - A = _____

21. A = 6, B = 15, C = 10, D = 5, E = 3

    (D + B + C) ÷ A = _____

22. A = 40, B = 37, C = 15, D = 10, E = 13

    B + E - D = _____

23. A = 3, B = 2, C = 90, D = 15, E = 4

    D x B x A = _____

24. A = 11, B 12, C = 66, D = 4, E = 24

    C ÷ A x D = _____

25. A = 7, B = 2, C = 8, D = 4, E = 12

    (A + E) - (C + D) = _____

26. A = 15, B = 6, C = 30, D = 9, E = 5

    (A + C) ÷ D = _____

Your colour rating....

Question 15		Question 16		Question 17		Question 18		Question 19		Question 20	
A	☐	A	☐	A	☐	A	☐	A	☐	A	☐
B	☐	B	☐	B	☐	B	☐	B	☐	B	☐
C	☐	C	☐	C	☐	C	☐	C	☐	C	☐
D	☐	D	☐	D	☐	D	☐	D	☐	D	☐
E	☐	E	☐	E	☐	E	☐	E	☐	E	☐

Question 21		Question 22		Question 23		Question 24		Question 25		Question 26	
A	☐	A	☐	A	☐	A	☐	A	☐	A	☐
B	☐	B	☐	B	☐	B	☐	B	☐	B	☐
C	☐	C	☐	C	☐	C	☐	C	☐	C	☐
D	☐	D	☐	D	☐	D	☐	D	☐	D	☐
E	☐	E	☐	E	☐	E	☐	E	☐	E	☐

Your score.... 26

Number Sequences

In each question, find the number that continues the sequence in the best way and mark it on the multiple choice answer sheet.

For example: 15,   25,   35,   45,   55,   **65**

1.   16, 20, 24, 28, 32

2.   9, 12, 15, 18, 21, 24

3.   6, 12, 24, 48, 96

4.   4, 12, 6, 13, 8, 14, 10, 15, 12

5.   10, 20, 25, 35, 40, 50, 55

6.   29, 26, 23, 20, 17

7.   800, 400, 200, 100,

8.   3, 9, 27, 81,

9.   50, 43, 36, 29, 22

10.   20, 80, 23, 76, 26, 72, 29, 68

11.   21, 23, 26, 30, 35, 41, 48

12.   26, 31, 36, 41, 46

13.   46, 39, 34, 27, 22, 15, 10

14.   98, 88, 79, 71, 64, 58, 53

15.   1, 4, 9, 16, 25, 36, 49

16.   15, 30, 45, 60, 75, 90

17.   30, 28, 60, 30, 120, 32, 240, 34

18.   1, 2, 3, 5, 7, 11, 13, 17, 19

19.   14, 16, 18, 21, 23, 25, 28, 30, 32

20.   20, 22, 19, 21, 18, 20, 17, 19, 16

21.   3, 4, 7, 11, 18, 29, 47

22.   1, 3, 7, 15, 31, 63

23.   29, 32, 36, 39, 43, 46, 50, 53

24.   76, 18, 72, 24, 68, 30, 64, 36, 60

25.   7, 18, 32, 43, 57, 68, 82

26.   11, 9, 14, 13, 17, 17, 20, 21, 23

Your colour rating....

Question 1	
34	
24	
40	
36	
26	

Question 2	
30	
27	
32	
28	
26	

Question 3	
180	
192	
144	
120	
100	

Question 4	
11	
14	
16	
20	
12	

Question 5	
65	
64	
60	
50	
75	

Question 6	
22	
14	
15	
24	
11	

Question 7	
75	
10	
90	
5	
50	

Question 8	
99	
236	
108	
252	
243	

Question 9	
20	
18	
15	
10	
9	

Question 10	
32	
64	
48	
37	
62	

Question 11	
60	
51	
65	
56	
54	

Question 12	
48	
41	
43	
51	
52	

Question 13	
3	
9	
6	
5	
7	

Question 14	
50	
49	
42	
36	
48	

Question 15	
64	
56	
42	
81	
100	

Question 16	
101	
95	
120	
110	
105	

Question 17	
36	
480	
440	
40	
500	

Question 18	
20	
25	
23	
6	
18	

Question 19	
34	
36	
35	
33	
42	

Question 20	
13	
20	
14	
18	
19	

Question 21	
80	
77	
72	
86	
76	

Question 22	
96	
84	
103	
127	
126	

Question 23	
57	
50	
58	
56	
59	

Question 24	
45	
27	
39	
18	
42	

Question 25	
96	
92	
86	
93	
88	

Question 26	
26	
24	
25	
22	
28	

Your score.... 26

Balancing Equations

For each of the questions below, find the missing number that completes the sum.

For example: 10 + 20 + 4 = 40 - 5 - (**1**)

1. 24 ÷ 6 x 8 = 70 - 10 - (   )

2. 21 x 2 - 7 = 28 ÷ 4 x (   )

3. 13 + 8 + 19 = 10 x 8 ÷ (   )

4. 25 x 3 - 10 = 15 + 40 + (   )

5. 67 - 17 - 8 = 9 x 8 - (   )

6. 42 ÷ 6 x 4 = 11 x 2 + (   )

7. 4 + 10 + 1 = 3 x 10 ÷ (   )

8. 7 x 8 - 11 = 30 ÷ 2 x (   )

9. 9 x 7 - 38 = 18 + 16 - (   )

10. 41 + 17 - 4 = 3 x 9 x (   )

11. 64 ÷ 8 x 3 = 7 + 14 + (   )

12. 10 + 15 + 5 = 10 - 3 + (   )

13. 40 ÷ 8 x 6 = 10 x 4 - (   )

14. 16 + 14 - 22 = 42 ÷ 3 - (   )

15. 60 ÷ 4 x 2 = 64 ÷ 2 - (   )

16. 6 x 7 + 10 = 4 x 9 + (   )

17. 49 ÷ 7 + 30 = 73 - 14 - (   )

18. 23 x 1 - 17 = 4 x 10 - (   )

19. 7 x 5 + 17 = 100 - 40 - (   )

20. 63 ÷ 9 x 10 = 25 x 4 - (   )

21. 62 - 25 - 12 = 81 ÷ 3 - (   )

22. 180 ÷ 6 - 10 = 96 ÷ 4 - (   )

23. 28 x 2 - 11 = 7 x 7 - (   )

24. 150 ÷ 15 x 4 = 76 - 19 - (   )

25. 96 ÷ 12 + 14 = 80 ÷ 4 + (   )

26. 17 x 3 - 6 = 5 x 5 + (   )

Your colour rating....

Question 1		Question 2		Question 3		Question 4		Question 5		Question 6	
28	☐	7	☐	6	☐	20	☐	20	☐	6	☐
32	☐	35	☐	2	☐	10	☐	22	☐	7	☐
60	☐	5	☐	4	☐	15	☐	28	☐	5	☐
26	☐	4	☐	8	☐	5	☐	30	☐	8	☐
30	☐	6	☐	3	☐	25	☐	34	☐	10	☐

Question 7		Question 8		Question 9		Question 10		Question 11		Question 12	
4	☐	6	☐	9	☐	2	☐	6	☐	22	☐
2	☐	7	☐	2	☐	10	☐	10	☐	12	☐
7	☐	2	☐	11	☐	5	☐	3	☐	16	☐
3	☐	5	☐	7	☐	3	☐	1	☐	23	☐
9	☐	3	☐	5	☐	6	☐	0	☐	24	☐

Question 13		Question 14		Question 15		Question 16		Question 17		Question 18	
10	☐	7	☐	3	☐	18	☐	20	☐	30	☐
30	☐	2	☐	9	☐	20	☐	32	☐	34	☐
20	☐	6	☐	14	☐	12	☐	13	☐	42	☐
15	☐	10	☐	6	☐	15	☐	22	☐	43	☐
12	☐	15	☐	2	☐	16	☐	16	☐	24	☐

Question 19		Question 20		Question 21		Question 22		Question 23		Question 24	
18	☐	29	☐	3	☐	4	☐	5	☐	13	☐
16	☐	30	☐	10	☐	60	☐	4	☐	17	☐
8	☐	24	☐	25	☐	8	☐	3	☐	19	☐
12	☐	32	☐	5	☐	2	☐	11	☐	21	☐
7	☐	33	☐	2	☐	30	☐	9	☐	18	☐

Question 25		Question 26	
6	☐	25	☐
20	☐	5	☐
14	☐	10	☐
2	☐	20	☐
18	☐	15	☐

Your score.... 26

Relating Numbers

In each of the questions below, the numbers in the third set of brackets must be related to each other in the same way as in the first two sets of brackets. Find the missing number for each question and mark it on the multiple choice answer sheet.

For example: (10 (17) 7)   (14 (25) 11)   (8 (**15**) 7)

1.   (17 (31) 14)   (9 (31) 22)   (15 (   ) 35)

2.   (8 (96) 12)   (4 (60) 15)   (20 (   ) 9)

3.   (135 (109) 26)   (58 (22) 36)   (77 (   ) 49)

4.   (7 (65) 9)   (11 (57) 5)   (14 (   ) 2)

5.   (38 (48) 11)   (22 (67) 46)   (10 (   ) 63)

6.   (6 (11) 48)   (8 (10) 56)   (4 (   ) 32)

7.   (12 (67) 6)   (3 (19) 8)   (7 (   ) 9)

8.   (29 (65) 32)   (27 (48) 17)   (10 (   ) 54)

9.   (19 (28) 37)   (23 (14) 5)   (35 (   ) 9)

10.   (20 (121) 131)   (100 (82) 172)   (30 (   ) 147)

11.   (7 (28) 2)   (3 (30) 5)   (4 (   ) 8)

12.   (84 (67) 32)   (45 (39) 21)   (27 (   ) 10)

Question 1	
40	☐
50	☐
70	☐
60	☐
80	☐

Question 2	
160	☐
180	☐
118	☐
120	☐
116	☐

Question 3	
38	☐
26	☐
35	☐
29	☐
28	☐

Question 4	
30	☐
25	☐
16	☐
31	☐
28	☐

Question 5	
87	☐
73	☐
79	☐
72	☐
62	☐

Question 6	
8	☐
9	☐
15	☐
11	☐
12	☐

Question 7	
63	☐
56	☐
60	☐
53	☐
58	☐

Question 8	
64	☐
72	☐
68	☐
58	☐
63	☐

Question 9	
26	☐
29	☐
14	☐
22	☐
32	☐

Question 10	
122	☐
127	☐
129	☐
117	☐
135	☐

Question 11	
24	☐
32	☐
48	☐
64	☐
56	☐

Question 12	
32	☐
27	☐
31	☐
17	☐
22	☐

Keep going.... There's more over the page!

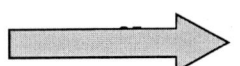

13. (2 (24) 6)   (4 (27) 5)   (2 (   ) 7)

14. (35 (10) 7)   (108 (17) 9)   (66 (   ) 6)

15. (3 (42) 15)   (12 (45) 4)   (7 (   ) 4)

16. (14 (41) 13)   (24 (66) 18)   (12 (   ) 19)

17. (8 (24) 6)   (5 (25) 10)   (7 (   ) 6)

18. (14 (77) 5)   (13 (85) 6)   (9 (   ) 12)

19. (11 (30) 28)   (56 (62) 15)   (17 (   ) 33)

20. (32 (104) 36)   (21 (59) 19)   (10 (   ) 25)

21. (15 (56) 4)   (9 (59) 7)   (8 (   ) 9)

22. (25 (95) 20)   (18 (95) 27)   (36 (   ) 14)

23. (5 (35) 3)   (4 (48) 7)   (3 (   ) 12)

24. (5 (72) 45)   (25 (24) 75)   (17 (   ) 34)

25. (113 (18) 100)   (92 (56) 41)   (42 (   ) 14)

26. (7 (59) 8)   (9 (84) 9)   (10 (   ) 6)

Your colour rating....

Question 13	
30	
15	
27	
9	
36	

Question 14	
11	
6	
16	
21	
17	

Question 15	
28	
22	
31	
26	
25	

Question 16	
40	
43	
24	
44	
29	

Question 17	
42	
20	
25	
40	
21	

Question 18	
112	
115	
108	
104	
113	

Question 19	
41	
59	
40	
51	
35	

Question 20	
70	
30	
60	
55	
65	

Question 21	
68	
70	
72	
74	
65	

Question 22	
90	
100	
115	
106	
110	

Question 23	
36	
45	
54	
56	
48	

Question 24	
2	
14	
16	
8	
24	

Question 25	
33	
43	
32	
41	
28	

Question 26	
43	
57	
60	
48	
63	

Your score....

Word Problems

Read the information for each question carefully, then find the correct answer and mark it on the answer sheet provided. You may be asked to mark down more than one answer for each question.

1. Maria's birthday is the 30th June. Jack's birthday is 6 days later. What date is Jack's birthday?

   _____

2. 5 animals are standing in a line. The lion is second from the end and to the right of the middle animal, which is a zebra. The animals on either end are a kangaroo and a tiger. The tortoise is to the right of the kangaroo. Who is furthest right?

   _____

3. Paul's dad is 5 times older than Paul will be next year. If Paul's Dad is 31 next year, how old is Paul now?

   _____

4. At lunchtimes, the classes of Gecko School go to the dinner hall to have their sandwiches. At midday, 40 children enter the dining room, but within 20 minutes, 17 leave to play outside, but another 30 enter at 12.30. By 12.45, there are only 16 children left. How many children left to play outside between 12.30 and 12.45?

   _____

5. Michael owns two bakeries. He works out that at one bakery, he needs 10 bags of flour to last for 7 days. How many bags of flour does he need for both bakeries to last for 4 weeks?

   _____

6. Ryan is going to be 10 in two years time. Jasmine is 6 years older than him, but one year younger than Yolanda. How old is Yolanda?

   _____

7. If the day before yesterday was Monday, what day will it be 3 days after tomorrow?

   _____

8. Callum, Victoria and Dinesh all had pizza for dinner. Victoria had salad and Callum had chips. Dinesh had chocolate ice cream for dessert while Victoria and Callum had apple pie.

   Which of the statements below MUST be true?

   A. Victoria and Callum shared a piece of apple pie.
   B. Dinesh had pizza, chips and apple pie.
   C. Victoria doesn't like chips.
   D. Callum had pizza, chips and apple pie.
   E. Dinesh had more chips than Callum.

   _____

9. Isabelle leaves for work everyday at 08.30, and her journey takes 25 minutes. Today she is late and when she arrives, her watch tells her the time is 09.45. However, it is 5 minutes fast. What time did she leave for work?

   _____

10. Josh is the youngest in his family. Jake is twice his age and will be 11 next year. Jennifer is seven years older than Josh. How old is Jennifer?

    _____

11. Holly, Edith, Rishin, Emily and Marcus all belong to chess club and play mini matches everyday.

    Holly, Rishin and Emily win 3 matches each on Monday.
    Marcus and Edith win 2 matches each on Tuesday.
    Rishin and Marcus win 4 matches each on Wednesday.
    Emily, Holly and Marcus win 2 matches each on Thursday.
    Rishin and Emily win 1 match each on Friday.

    Which two people have won the same number of matches this week?

    _____ and _____

Question 1	
24th June	☐
26th June	☐
5th July	☐
3rd July	☐
6th July	☐

Question 2	
kangaroo	☐
tortoise	☐
lion	☐
zebra	☐
tiger	☐

Question 3	
5	☐
6	☐
8	☐
10	☐
7	☐

Question 4	
27	☐
47	☐
33	☐
37	☐
29	☐

Question 5	
100	☐
40	☐
20	☐
70	☐
80	☐

Question 6	
14	☐
8	☐
17	☐
15	☐
16	☐

Question 7	
Sunday	☐
Monday	☐
Saturday	☐
Thursday	☐
Tuesday	☐

Question 8	
A	☐
B	☐
C	☐
D	☐
E	☐

Question 9	
09.25	☐
09.15	☐
09.10	☐
09.05	☐
09.20	☐

Question 10	
13	☐
17	☐
5	☐
11	☐
12	☐

Question 11	
Holly	☐
Edith	☐
Rishin	☐
Emily	☐
Marcus	☐

Keep going.... There's more over the page!

12. Kieran is going to be 14 next year. His older sister Nicola is 10 years older than him. How old was Nicola two years ago?

    _____

13. 5 children are in a running race at school. Rhiannon finishes before Skye but after Anneka. Bella is faster than Anneka and Harry is the slowest. Who finishes in 4th place?

    _____

14. Molly gets on a train at 09.20 and arrives at her stop 50 minutes later. She plans to meet her friend Tom for a hot chocolate 5 minutes after her train arrives, but Tom arrives 7 minutes late. What time do they meet?

    _____

15. Pete, Matt, Andy, Reina and Gary are counting the number of planes they see over 5 days.

    Day 1 - Matt and Andy both saw 2, but Reina saw 1
    Day 2 - Gary, Pete and Reina both saw 2
    Day 3 - Andy saw 3
    Day 4 - Reina, Matt and Gary saw 2 each
    Day 5 - Pete saw 3 more than Matt who only saw 1

    Who saw the most planes over the 5 days?

    _____

16. Marissa and Roxanne are having a 16th birthday party together. In the first hour, 39 people arrive. In the second hour, 4 people leave but another 11 arrive. At the end of the evening, there are 20 people left. If no-one else arrived, how many people left after the second hour?

    _____

17. On one shift, a zookeeper is looking after 5 monkeys. One monkey eats a maximum of 3 bananas an hour. What is the maximum number of bananas all 5 monkeys could eat in 3 hours?

    _____

18. A number of schools are playing in a tournament. In the first game, Mildmay score five goals against St John's, who lose by two. In the second game, Newlands beat Lawford Mead by one goal, even though the losing team scored four. How many goals had been scored altogether?

    _____

19. Siobhan is 3 years younger than Rachel. Rachel is 12 years older than Richard who was 6 last year. How old is Siobhan?

    _____

20. At Iguana School, lessons are 1 hour long. There are 5 lessons each day. School starts at 09.00, with a break of 15 minutes after the second lesson. There is then another lesson and then lunch, which is 1 hour 15 minutes long. What time do students finish school?

    _____

21. 5 folders stand lined up on a shelf, each a different colour. The blue folder is to the right of the pink folder, and two spaces to the left of the white folder. The green folder is the middle folder and the black folder is to the right of the white folder. Which folder is furthest left?

    _____

Your colour rating....

Question 12	
20	☐
21	☐
23	☐
25	☐
19	☐

Question 13	
Rhiannon	☐
Skye	☐
Anneka	☐
Bella	☐
Harry	☐

Question 14	
10.15	☐
10.22	☐
10.17	☐
10.20	☐
10.25	☐

Question 15	
Pete	☐
Matt	☐
Andy	☐
Reina	☐
Gary	☐

Question 16	
20	☐
21	☐
30	☐
24	☐
26	☐

Question 17	
15	☐
40	☐
45	☐
30	☐
25	☐

Question 18	
17	☐
19	☐
15	☐
12	☐
14	☐

Question 19	
12	☐
16	☐
3	☐
15	☐
19	☐

Question 20	
03.30	☐
16.30	☐
15.00	☐
15.30	☐
13.30	☐

Question 21	
blue	☐
pink	☐
white	☐
green	☐
black	☐

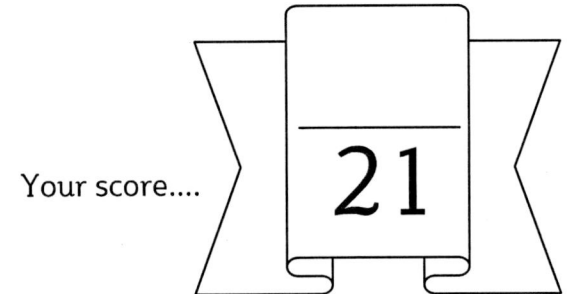

Your score.... 21

Answers

Letter Sequences Answers

1. PI
2. OC
3. NA
4. PZ
5. ZJ
6. KA
7. EK
8. KB
9. OP
10. PK
11. JY
12. SQ
13. GV
14. YG
15. IU
16. XF
17. BD
18. AQ
19. DK
20. LP
21. DV
22. PX
23. KS
24. KI
25. WL
26. XV

Letter Analogies Answers

1. SU
2. BV
3. AO
4. NV
5. QJ
6. PI
7. PF
8. QS
9. XD
10. KG
11. SX
12. WR
13. OK
14. GN
15. CX
16. BZ
17. LT
18. TS
19. XN
20. FK
21. BG
22. OJ
23. CD
24. WI
25. AO
26. EL

Code Words Answers

1. GPSGO
2. MCABN
3. VWXGB
4. BIN
5. TJHIU
6. CINEMA
7. MAGIC
8. LAMJU
9. ZCFGLB
10. XLEVI
11. CHANCE
12. FIRST
13. KLHGVI
14. YHKZBOX
15. XVYXL
16. ALWAYS
17. SUMMER
18. IYTYIC
19. ALIVE
20. BEACH
21. IWNSP
22. MARCH
23. MONKEY
24. QXHBK
25. WIDGK
26. XSROW

Word Formation Answers

1. orb
2. rat
3. lean
4. pear
5. mead
6. nerd
7. sail
8. ears
9. pace
10. beep
11. wigs
12. heirs
13. pies
14. clan
15. oars
16. arts
17. fist
18. arch
19. hares
20. lock
21. ream
22. leap
23. rove
24. rant
25. sake
26. else

Word Formation 2 Answers

1. pile
2. teal
3. nice
4. call
5. soars
6. eels
7. life
8. deal
9. hour
10. steer
11. sail
12. tree
13. moat
14. sign
15. mane
16. lead
17. plea
18. roar
19. dice
20. name
21. bead
22. pest
23. stay
24. seal
25. rile
26. ales

Code Matching Answers

1. 632468
2. 74368
3. TRACE
4. FOAL
5. 3225
6. LOAF
7. 185524
8. MATE
9. 4352
10. 5267
11. MERRY
12. FRAME
13. MUDDLE
14. 4557
15. RULE
16. NEEDLE
17. LIME
18. 692468
19. 47596
20. DRAKE
21. REALLY
22. 4367
23. PRAM
24. LIAR
25. 56257
26. DREAD
27. 362257

Missing Letters Answers

1. T
2. R
3. H
4. M
5. L
6. K
7. G
8. P
9. K
10. F
11. W
12. H
13. T
14. E
15. T
16. D
17. S
18. G
19. B
20. Y
21. E
22. M
23. H
24. A
25. T
26. B

Hidden Words Answers

1. until everything (tile)
2. that ripe (trip)
3. new stereo (news)
4. is late (slat)
5. that wine (twin)
6. Tom bought (tomb)
7. new hens (when)
8. bit every (bite)
9. car down (card)
10. Sarah and (hand)
11. will order (lord)
12. after my (term)
13. the irises (heir)
14. to escape (toes)
15. taxis leave (isle)
16. Peter opened (rope)
17. ask impossible (skim)
18. hero began (robe)
19. through industry (hind)
20. him any (many)
21. hospital kiosk (talk)
22. too lucky (tool)
23. threw all (wall)
24. are a (area)
25. each evening (ache)
26. piano seems (nose)

Transferring Letters Answers

1. G
2. P
3. R
4. U
5. T
6. G
7. H
8. C
9. T
10. C
11. R
12. C
13. N
14. E
15. B
16. L
17. O
18. T
19. F
20. G
21. R
22. R
23. I
24. O
25. H
26. F

Odd Ones Out Answers

1. painting, statue
2. broccoli, pea
3. Africa, Europe
4. deer, cow
5. cube, cylinder
6. beach, stalk
7. vile, feeble
8. teacher, lesson
9. paper, book
10. smile, laugh
11. top, middle
12. forgive, pardon
13. occupied, full
14. foot, print
15. soul, numerous
16. cousin, relative
17. sow, mare
18. mouth, hear
19. similar, alike
20. ill, spot
21. flower, tree
22. sock, shoe
23. Venus, Saturn
24. sail, lake
25. criminal, thief
26. warehouse, office

Synonyms Answers

1. dangerous, hazardous
2. fatigued, exhausted
3. vicar, priest
4. loan, lend
5. thoughtful, considerate
6. dinghy, boat
7. severe, grave
8. close, near
9. earth, soil
10. laugh, chuckle
11. cookie, biscuit
12. light, bright
13. puzzle, riddle
14. plumage, feathers
15. obey, comply
16. divide, split
17. cease, halt
18. clap, applaud
19. fool, trick
20. experiment, trial
21. defeat, vanquish
22. injured, hurt
23. statue, sculpture
24. dinner, supper
25. sight, vision
26. core, centre

Antonyms Answers

1. many, few
2. departure, arrival
3. hide, reveal
4. alert, tired
5. loathe, love
6. hope, despair
7. thin, obese
8. deny, admit
9. assemble, dismantle
10. rise, plummet
11. coarse, smooth
12. cowardly, brave
13. forbid, allow
14. dear, inexpensive
15. strength, weakness
16. sharp, blunt
17. futile, worthwhile
18. entire, partial
19. uphold, abolish
20. advance, retreat
21. opaque, transparent
22. deliberate, accidental
23. reluctant, eager
24. scatter, collect
25. find, lose
26. create, destroy

Compound Words Answers	Complete the Word Answers	Homonyms Answers
1. sun, shine	1. EAT	1. pen
2. table, cloth	2. RAN	2. fine
3. hope, fully	3. HER	3. fan
4. mess, age	4. RED	4. safe
5. play, ground	5. AMP	5. can
6. be, an	6. CUP	6. handle
7. any, where	7. BAT	7. palm
8. goose, berry	8. RIB	8. bank
9. scare, crow	9. OFF	9. blind
10. consider, able	10. MAN	10. green
11. plea, sure	11. USE	11. track
12. sauce, pan	12. GIN	12. right
13. with, draw	13. CAT	13. ring
14. under, mine	14. LOG	14. watch
15. over, look	15. MET	15. stick
16. work, shop	16. LAY	16. space
17. eye, lid	17. RAN	17. pitch
18. man, kind	18. APT	18. pass
19. rat, her	19. GUM	19. plant
20. ham, mock	20. OLD	20. clog
21. for, tune	21. ACT	21. wood
22. so, up	22. KIN	22. foot
23. in, finite	23. RAT	23. land
24. excel, led	24. COG	24. bear
25. go, at	25. AND	25. train
26. know, ledge	26. EAT	26. board

Sentence Analogies Answers	Algebra Answers	Number Sequences Answers
1. hear, see	1. A	1. 36
2. calf, foal	2. E	2. 27
3. April, May	3. D	3. 192
4. dough, wood	4. B	4. 16
5. artist, composer	5. E	5. 65
6. fish, bird	6. B	6. 14
7. leaf, petal	7. A	7. 50
8. bright, breadth	8. D	8. 243
9. cattle, lions	9. D	9. 15
10. clock, calendar	10. B	10. 32
11. stones, kilometres	11. A	11. 56
12. dog, horse	12. B	12. 51
13. ten, hundred	13. A	13. 3
14. dock, hangar	14. B	14. 49
15. arrow, racquet	15. B	15. 64
16. herb, spice	16. E	16. 105
17. fall, leap	17. C	17. 480
18. envy, anger	18. E	18. 23
19. bacon, mutton	19. A	19. 35
20. pessimist, strong	20. E	20. 18
21. queen, actress	21. D	21. 76
22. clear, clouded	22. A	22. 127
23. blue, green	23. C	23. 57
24. hive, byre	24. E	24. 42
25. loan, pane	25. A	25. 93
26. hand, foot	26. E	26. 25

Balancing Equations Answers	Relating Numbers Answers	Word Problems Answers
1. 28	1. 50	1. 6th July
2. 5	2. 180	2. tiger
3. 2	3. 28	3. 5
4. 10	4. 30	4. 37
5. 30	5. 72	5. 80
6. 6	6. 11	6. 15
7. 2	7. 58	7. Sunday
8. 3	8. 68	8. D
9. 9	9. 22	9. 09.15
10. 2	10. 127	10. 12
11. 3	11. 64	11. Rishin and Marcus
12. 23	12. 32	12. 21
13. 10	13. 27	13. Skye
14. 6	14. 16	14. 10.22
15. 2	15. 25	15. Pete
16. 16	16. 43	16. 26
17. 22	17. 21	17. 45
18. 34	18. 115	18. 17
19. 8	19. 41	19. 16
20. 30	20. 60	20. 15.30
21. 2	21. 68	21. pink
22. 4	22. 100	
23. 4	23. 56	
24. 17	24. 16	
25. 2	25. 33	
26. 20	26. 63	